THE CONCEPTION MANDALA

MARK OLSEN and SAMUEL AVITAL

DESTINY BOOKS
ROCHESTER, VERMONT

Destiny Books
One Park Street
Rochester, Vermont 05767

LIBRARY OF CONGRESS CATALOGING-IN-PUBLICATION DATA

Olsen, Mark, 1954–
The conception mandala : creative techniques for inviting a child into your life / Mark Olsen and Samuel Avital.
p. cm.
Includes index.
ISBN 0-89281-356-3
1. Conception—Miscellanea. 2. Sex—Miscellanea. 3. Pregnancy—Miscellanea. I. Avital, Samuel. II. Title.
BF 1999.0427 1992
155.6'46—dc20 92–4921
CIP

Text design by Randi Jinkins

Printed and bound in the United States

10 9 8 7 6 5 4 3 2 1

Destiny Books is a division of Inner Traditions International, Ltd.

Distributed to the book trade in the United States by American International Distribution Corporation (AIDC)

Distributed to the book trade in Canada by Book Center, Inc., Montreal, Quebec

*We would like to thank Leslie Colket
and the editing staff at Inner Traditions
International for their hard work and attention
to detail. Special thanks to Jeremy and Rachel
for their pioneering spirits in this work.
Last but not least, Mr. Olsen wishes to
thank his wife, Jane, and his son, Benjamin,
both of whom provide constant reminders of the
joys of living consciously.*

CONTENTS

INTRODUCTION

Anyone who has ever seen childbirth and witnessed the radiance of a newborn must surely recognize the great miracle of this event. The presence of a tiny person fresh from the womb and full of pure innocence touches us to the very core of our beings. Even so, we tend to forget that long before the event of birth, another event occurred that was equally amazing.

This book was written to reconfirm the wondrous qualities of that process we call conception. It was also written to remind us that we participate in the creation of our own reality, and, as such, we should take responsibility for the manner in which we bring new human beings to this earth. This book suggests a sane and conscious way of bringing a generation of healthy and integrated human beings into the world.

What you are holding is a manual that can help parents embrace this responsibility. It is a guidebook to conscious conception, a means whereby we can interact with subtle energies and participate in the process of attracting beings who will come to us according to the noblest aims of their individual consciousness.

The birth of every living thing is indeed special. It signifies the ongoing process of renewal. Endowed as we are with reflective consciousness, the birth of one of our own species is a particularly thrilling occasion. Our society often honors the occasion with ritual expressions of love and celebration. Neighbors bring food for the weary parents, family members travel—sometimes great distances—in order to see, hold, and coo at the baby, and nearly everyone sends a card to congratulate the parents on their new arrival. Other cultures have developed dances, songs, and events to signal the arrival of a new member of the family.

This same reflective consciousness has stimulated and supported our curiosity about the conception process. Science, the formal extension of our natural curiosity, has managed to reveal the procreative process as a series of biological events. While it is important to know the reliable components of the process in all its microscopic glory, it is equally important to recognize and interact with the invisible forces guiding the process.

Every philosophy or religious ideology strives to reconcile the presence of the ineffable with the concrete. That has always been the essential work of artists, sages, and people of conscience. In light of this, modern men and women should recognize and embrace the very real responsibilities associated with all facets of conception.

Common sense dictates that the conditions of conception must in some way influence the entry of a soul into this plane of existence. This belief is reflected in many of the courtship, fertility, and premarital rituals used by cultures throughout history.

The ancient Greeks, for example, used sacred groves as courtship gardens. Couples preparing for marriage were encouraged to stroll together, no doubt finding various spots among the greenery and sculpture to express their desires.

Off and on throughout China's history there have existed practices of presenting to newlyweds suggestive artwork, lovemaking manuals called pillowbooks, and pictures of cuddly babies—rituals said to provide both magical and friendly support for the couple's fertility.

Various Brazilian Macumba sects offer special services designed to positively influence the aspects of conception. Using chants, ritual drumming, and dance, the woman is guided into a trance during which she may receive the blessings of a particular deity thought to be beneficial in bringing forth healthy, happy children.

At wedding parties medieval Europeans were allowed

to tease newlyweds with bawdy, suggestive language. This practice was considered useful as a means of banishing the "evil eye" and promoting a successful coupling.

Astrologers in all cultures have been employed by couples seeking advice about their conception timing. Aligning with the various movements of the planets during coition is believed to enhance the destiny of the child and, therefore, the parents.

We invite the reader to use the methods supplied in this book. These methods are updated and simplified versions of time-tested techniques drawn from the ancient traditions. If you have solid training in a particular religion or spiritual discipline, you may certainly transfer the essential ingredients of this work to your own context. It is important, however, to distill the essence of the information and not simply its form.

The purpose of this book is to offer a new, culturally neutral approach to this beautiful human process of conception. We contend that the kaleidoscope of cultural traditions, although fascinating, is too often a hindrance to the more direct and genuine authority of the individual human being. Although the honest and creative efforts of each individual may indeed match certain customs, we believe in the effectiveness of those efforts that grow out of the creative power within each person. This self-reliance builds maturity and strength and ultimately increases happiness.

For a variety of reasons, a couple might find themselves

in the position of wanting to adopt a child. In this instance, much of the data included in this manual will still apply. Certain adjustments must obviously be made to accommodate the notion of the child coming to you through a nontraditional selection process—one that is no less responsive to the energy of love than the traditional one. A couple wishing to adopt must abide by the conditions of the adoption, yet, through the exercises in this book, they can grow as prospective parents and welcome the visions they have of the child they sense will come to them.

One of the simplest and most effective tools available to you in any endeavor is your own inner vision. The power of the mind's eye has long been used to heal, clarify, and inspire artists, composers, athletes, and people from all walks of life. Many sections of this book contain meditation or visualization exercises to clarify motives, support the efforts of both partners, and establish the foundation for conscious conception.

Using one's inner vision can enhance the birth process as well. If both parents visualize a healthy, joyful birth experience and, at the same time, commit to maintaining good prenatal care, the chances for a safe, fulfilling experience are considerably higher.

If you are truly motivated to use this manual in a practical way, our first suggestion is that you and your partner immediately begin to work with the materials in the order provided. Later, after completing the exercises in this book, you may want to consult individual chapters for a deeper understanding or for quick reference.

With all of this in mind, let us embark upon a daring adventure together. We dedicate this work to all who cherish the uniqueness of the individual and celebrate the power of that individual to brighten our world.

1

THE NOTEBOOKS

Throughout the conscious conception process, each partner is instructed to keep a personal notebook to record thoughts, feelings, and other important information gleaned from the experience. A third notebook—the master notebook—will contain the partners' combined writings and sections chosen from their personal notebooks. The master notebook is intended to eventually become the property of the child.

We rarely take time to appreciate the powerful ability to formulate abstract thought and put it into words. This ability is partially responsible for the development of human consciousness. Consider that lightning-quick brain waves flying past at incredible speeds can be captured by the conscious act of writing. Once caught, they can be refined and reflected upon for deeper, more metaphorical layers of thought.

Captured thoughts have a curious way of grouping together to form ideas. These ideas eventually organize into larger groups called concepts. Any number of concepts can also unite into powerful new shapes that cannot help but trigger the deep resources of the body and mind.

Grouping thoughts into grammatical units and writing them onto a sheet of paper gives them resonance, clarity, and a certain amount of conceptual shaping. Waves of thought are tamed just long enough to travel along specific lines, deepening the shape and meaning of the lines with each reading and carving an impression onto the soul. Writing, therefore, is one very useful way of reformulating and recharging thoughts in a manner that can actually affect the physical world. Unlike most fleeting thoughts, deeply charged impressions more readily lead to action. They also provide a reliable basis for discernment as the individual selects actions from the vast array of possibilities.

Bringing a child into the world in a conscious way is a formidable creative act. It matches the courage and risk of all great art. It stimulates our highest perceptions and gives rise to great leaps of creativity. One very important aspect of all creativity, however, is grounding. An artist well grounded in technique has the freedom to go beyond it; a dancer grounded in the daily fundamentals of dance can truly embody music; a tree with strong roots can grow to great heights.

The notebooks in this work serve as the necessary grounding device. A strong commitment to working with the notebooks throughout the conception process will support your creative endeavor with all of its ups and downs. In short, the written word will help keep the imagination honest.

If you are someone for whom the idea of writing rings old alarms of insecurity or fear related to past attempts, take heart: Being a writer has little to do with the function of your notebook. The form of your entries is not dictated by conventional rules of writing. On the contrary, the only rule is that you allow the words to arise simply and sincerely from an honest place within yourself.

If you have a facility for writing, this process will be somewhat easier. What you must watch out for, however, is the temptation to overwrite. Remember that less is more.

THE PURPOSE OF THE NOTEBOOKS

Each partner should purchase his or her own notebook of an appealing size and color. Feel free to open the floodgates in your individual notebooks and write as though no one else will read your words—for no one will unless you so choose.

The selection of the master notebook might be more difficult because it should have a special quality and be agreeable to both partners in color, size, and feel. The creation of the master notebook as a gift for the child endows it with added significance. It is a storage bank of energy, feelings, and values that will one day powerfully resonate in the awareness of the invited child.

Like all things of power, the master notebook should be passed to the child when he or she is ready to receive it, perhaps in early adolescence, late teens, or early adulthood. The notebook should be accompanied by an explanation, and, if possible, it should be passed in the presence of both parents.

THE PROCESS

The impressions and data accumulated by doing the exercises in this book provide a wealth of information that may be useful for focusing on the specifics of the statements outlined below. We suggest recording initial responses and then filling out or altering them after working through the exercises.

Organizational formats we suggest refer primarily to the master notebook. The creation of the master notebook provides a reconciliation factor and an objective basis whereby the data of the two individual notebooks can be merged. Individual notebooks are entirely self-styled and free-form in nature, although master notebook suggestions may certainly be adopted if desired.

Complete the following statements in the individual notebooks, writing freely and without judgment. It might be helpful to adhere to the structure of the master notebook, which will unfold in the order described, although any form is good as long as the information is recorded.

Statement of Intent

Each partner writes down his or her personal motives for wanting to bring a child into the world. The length of the statement of intent is not important, although we recommend writing at least two paragraphs. Remember that this book is a guide to completing these statements and that the exercises should be carried out and the experiences recorded in the individual notebooks before formulating a final version for the master notebook.

It is usually a good idea to start with your obvious intentions and those related to your love for your partner. Then let yourself search deeper to find those other motives aligned with your highest aims. It is perfectly all right to sound lofty or poetic at this stage. It is equally acceptable to sound pragmatic and simple, just as long as you remain true to yourself.

A typical entry might incorporate any of the following concepts, as well as countless others:

- The sharing of love with a new being
- The need for self-growth and discovery through parenting
- The desire to nurture in a healthy environment
- The desire to experience the dynamics of family life

Feel free to include details and to be creative. The statement will have greater power if it comes from deep within you.

The Invitation

The invitation should be a warm and heartfelt statement inviting a new being into your home, into your family, and into your life. Specifics of this invitation are developed through the exercises contained in this book. When developing the invitation for the master notebook, do not be surprised if it takes several versions to arrive at an invitation that meets the needs of both partners.

The invitation is described in greater detail in Chapter 4. Generally speaking, however, all good invitations have elements of charm and promise. They express the readiness of the parents to receive a new arrival into their lives. The invitation is written in your own vernacular and incorporates heartfelt feelings, enthusiasm, humor, and humility.

Description of Attributes

Record any physical and nonphysical characteristics of the child you wish to invite. Include all aspects that are intuitively felt as well as items that are more objectively desired. This is similar to the way in which an artist will play with renderings of a portrait until the right image emerges. Much like the artist, you are creating a visualized portrait.

Important self-discoveries often surface at this point. You might discover that you have a preference for the sex of the child. Perhaps you wish the child to inherit your temperament or your spouse's hair color and so forth. All desirable attributes should be freely admitted and recorded as they come to you. Gradually, through a process of addition and subtraction, you will begin to derive a composite of the kind of person you hope to invite into your family.

This does not suggest, of course, that you have the power to select a child the way you might order a meal. Rather, this technique moves you to consult your instincts in terms of probabilities while also helping you to determine the qualities in yourself and your partner that you hope to pass on to the child. While the preference for certain physical traits may seem prejudicial, it is only by recognizing our preferences and expectations that we can examine them openly.

At this stage of the exercise, all attributes should be positive. Concentrate exclusively on the qualities you most admire. Some of the obvious categories to consider are facial features, body type, basic temperament, intellect, relationship to the outside world, and state of health.

When your composite is complete, you must perform what often proves to be a difficult task: You must look at these positive aspects and consider their opposites or contraries. Our world is a dynamic interplay of polar opposites, and any being incarnated into this world is functioning under those basic conditions. Therefore, every positive attribute for which you wish will be accompanied by its opposite in some form.

That is not to say that the positive will not dominate, only that you should come to terms with the inevitable play of opposites and be willing to accept this person as a whole being. Moreover, it is important to recognize that you will love and care for this child unconditionally.

After considering the physical and nonphysical attributes of the child you wish to invite, incorporate your descriptions into a single comprehensive statement. Use your individual notebooks to work through the feelings you have generated, and then write a combined statement for the master notebook.

Statement of Welcome

Once the final versions of the statement of intent, the invitation, and the description of attributes are recorded in the master notebook, both partners should team up to create a statement of welcome for the child. This statement is a loving and personal act that, through poetic or narrative means, signifies the open hearts and loving arms of both parents. It is comforting for a child who is coming of age to read that he or she was welcomed into the home. How many children really get to hear that they were wanted and loved from the beginning?

The value of writing an early statement of welcome is that when you are busy dealing with the many adjustments needed to accommodate a new arrival, it will already be written and ready to read as the baby rests in your loving arms. On the other hand, the intensity of feelings at birth may be conducive to more profound and heartfelt statements of welcome. In addition, the growth process associated with pregnancy further contributes to the creation of insights that might not have been extant in the early stages of writing the statement. Therefore, think of this welcome statement as a work in progress, one that might go through several variations as your awareness grows and deepens with the unfolding experience.

CREATING THE MASTER NOTEBOOK

While working through the exercises in this book and developing the individual versions of the statement of intent, the invitation, and the description of attributes, the two of you must forge a third version of each statement that marries your individual notebooks. This project can be one of the most beautiful explorations any couple can make together. There will inevitably be points of disagreement, but the process of finding shared solutions can serve as a useful bonding agent for years to come. It is a process that should be viewed as friendly, but also one that demands honesty from both yourself and your partner.

Both partners should feel free to transfer selected entries from their individual notebooks into the master notebook throughout the conception process. In this way, each partner maintains his or her privacy and yet has a forum for sharing ideas. The master notebook can continue to grow, even throughout the pregnancy.

Creating and maintaining a notebook is understandably easier for first-time parents. Schedules get packed once a child is born, and there are endless new responsibilities. Nevertheless, it is such important work that we strongly urge parents to commit themselves to it with each child. The rewards of building this progression of conscious parenting are surely worth the inconvenience.

The Story of the Birth

The final section of the master notebook should be called the Story of the Birth. As the title implies, this portion of the notebook is for recording the details of the birth. It is good to start with the basic facts, such as the exact location of the birth, the length of labor, the time and style of delivery, names of those present, birth weight, and so forth. Afterwards, include anecdotes, impressions, thoughts and feelings at the time, and any and all pertinent details to help paint the full picture of the event.

Once this section is completed, the notebook work is finished. Ultimately, the notebooks stand as a testament to the degree of love, care, and consciousness that went into the conception of your child. They can also serve as a model for when the child has grown and may be considering having a family. This practice could help create a bonding element within the family for generations.

SUMMARY OF NOTEBOOK PREPARATION

1. Select the individual notebooks. Begin to record dreams, feelings, hopes for the future, etc.
2. Select the master notebook.
3. In the individual notebooks, write the following statements:
   a. Statement of intent
   b. The invitation
   c. Description of attributes
4. Create combined versions of each statement and record them in the master notebook.
5. Create a combined statement of welcome and record it in the master notebook.
6. Return to the individual notebooks and record anything that pertains to the conception process. Continue throughout the pregnancy, recording select portions into the master notebook as appropriate.
7. Leave a final section of the master notebook to be called the Story of the Birth. Record details of the birth event in the master notebook soon after the birth.
8. Present master notebook to child at appropriate time.

2

MANDALA: THE UNIVERSAL CIRCLE

The circle is one of the essential shapes of creation; it represents nothing less than life itself. Breath, for example, is a circular pattern of inhalation and exhalation; the moon provides nightly variations on a circular theme; the seasons are circular cycles; and the eyes, those glorious optic windows to our souls, are, of course, circular. Throughout history, humans have relied on the shape of the circle to represent both the time-bound realities of life and the timeless qualities of the spirit.

One of the most inspired representations of this idea is the circular design called a mandala. A mandala is usually a two-dimensional artwork that incorporates symbolic and optic qualities into a circle for the purpose of recording information or to provide a springboard for self-reflection.

The word *mandala* is Sanskrit and means sacred circle. It is often associated with the Hindu and Buddhist representations of the sacred lotus flower. Although the word has Eastern origins, mandalas can be found in the iconography of nearly every world religion. Consider the great Aztec calendar stone, for example, or Navajo sand paintings, the Rose Window at the Cathedral of Chartres, Tibetan yantra paintings, or the ground plans of nearly every holy shrine.

Mandalas even occur as basic structural symbols in our deepest dreams. Psychologist Carl Jung, credited with advancing the notion of a collective unconscious, made the study of mandalas a key element in his work with dreams. Taking clues from the Tibetan tradition of high priests who created elaborate wheels of symbolic information through the use of their active imagination, Professor Jung began to explore the possibility that this universal shape did not just spring forth spontaneously from a Tibetan priest.

After carefully studying the dreams of over four hundred patients, Jung came to believe that the mandala shape was quite possibly an archetype representing the center of the personality not identified with the ego. For Jung, the mandala was not a singular cultural phenomenon but a symbol that originated in the dreams and visions of all people in all cultures.

In our everyday lives we experience the circle as the shape of the arms in a loving embrace, the circle of family and friends, the concentric rings of still water disturbed by a pebble, the rotation of day to night and night to day, the eyes of a loved one. It is no surprise that, at some point in history, we created sacred circles to express these and other similar experiences that seem too elusive or mysterious to express any other way.

The sacred circle is clearly an important instrument that has been used by seekers and sages throughout history. While the practical uses of the mandala vary from tradition to tradition and age to age, its use as a tool for contemplation and self-examination has remained constant.

It is in this context that we have found the mandala to be particularly well suited for work with conscious conception. The mandala provides a way in which to express and clarify the process of bringing a being into your life. Unlike the practice of the Tibetan priest, who takes traditional religious ideas from the outer world and uses them to construct a very specialized inner mandala apparent only to the mind's eye, the use of the mandala in the conception process is designed to evoke inner ideas and bring them out in a form that can be appreciated by both partners.

Although the process is reversed, we feel the result is no less meaningful than that achieved by the Tibetan priest. Constructing a mandala is a meditation and a powerful clarifying agent, allowing partners to honor their own and each other's dreams, aims, and tastes and merge them into a single unified shape, sweeping clear deep layers of confusion. The mandala provides a format for expressing deep feelings, sharing new hopes, and making clear choices. It gives the couple a project to work on that directly relates to the experience of conceiving a child. And finally, the mandala project represents a shared process and unified result, reflecting the same forces inherent in every aspect of creation.

Once completed, the mandala becomes, among other things, a focusing device for the couple as they navigate their path amid the maelstrom of life choices; it becomes a visualization guide to enhance metaphorical thinking and the ability to take action; it becomes a precious heirloom of the heart representing deep parental love.

There are numerous projects that all couples complete to prepare for a new arrival. The construction of a mandala, a project unfettered by convention and rooted in the dedication to honest and constructive values, can have an enormous impact on the relationship of the parents to each other and to the newly arrived family member.

We suggest that both partners experience some of the exercises described in this book before making your first mandala. The exercises will provide fresh insight and useful data necessary for making clear, creative choices. Keep track of your feelings and insights in your individual notebooks.

MANDALA SHAPES

The following pages contain a series of basic mandala shapes. Within the descriptions we have included suggestions for arranging the visual data to allow for maximum effect. Each shape has its own flavor, so to speak, but they all function with equal power. Look them over until you settle on a shape that both partners agree meets your particular needs; then refer to the instructions for making your own conception mandala.

The mandala in Figure 1 (page 27) has a certain architectural formality. It seems practical and well suited to imagery that is realistic in nature. It is very close in shape to the Native American medicine wheel, which has practical restorative functions. The clearly defined rectangles lend themselves to four distinct aspects of life. The mandala could easily be organized for such categories as career, home, family, and romance; travel, health, education, and money; or any combination of these.

The mandala in Figure 2 (page 28) has great optic possibilities. It could be seen as a construct of alternating triangular patterns, depending upon the color scheme and the imagery. The patterns compete, interrelate, unfold, and generally stimulate the eye to invent new ways to view the whole.

The mandala in Figure 3 (page 29) maintains the outer rim for referencing and then moves into a more abstract format. Note that the shape is designed on the recurring pattern of the number four. A solid dot alters the center circle, forcing the imagery to flow around it. This shape would benefit from a bold use of color.

The mandala in Figure 4 (page 30) is a useful shape for organizing areas of life experience. The 12 sections might represent separate aspects of one's life; the rim could be used to link them all together. The center circle might be used to place a central image, perhaps a photo of the couple.

For those whose belief systems include astrology, this mandala is an ideal shape to organize images according to the houses of the zodiac. The mandala is divided into 12 equal sections, with a concentric rim around the whole. This rim allows for the placement of identifying symbols to record both the number of the section and the ruling planet. It could also accommodate additional information about the specific nature of each of the 12 sections.

Traditionally, the first section or house as it is called by astrologers, is the one just below the horizontal line drawn at the nine-o'clock position. From there the houses number counterclockwise.

Split into hemispheres, the circle reveals more generalized references to experience. The upper hemisphere of the circle, for example, generally represents one's life in the outer world; the lower hemisphere is seen to represent the inner world. The left hemisphere is said to represent the areas in life directed by will. The right, then, represents the path of surrender or "going with the flow."

Within each hemisphere, the houses reflect specific areas of experience. Those of you familiar with astrological charts will recognize, for example, the third house as the house of communication and mental activity; the seventh house as the house of marriage, partnerships, and contracts; and the tenth house as the house of career, achievement, and recognition.

If you are unfamiliar with the astrological system and wish to pursue it in more detail, consult one of the many books on astrology.

The mandala in Figure 5 (page 31) may be used as a modified zodiac wheel. It can also handle images and information that become increasingly specialized, increasingly private, or increasingly intense. The center circle is an ideal place to put a core image.

The classic design shown in Figure 6 (page 32) also has optic qualities. This one, however, has the added advantage of ordering the imagery in ever-increasing levels of importance. One could, for example, choose to have the bull's-eye as the primary area of focus; or one could view the material as developing outward, leaving the outer ring as the primary area of focus. The rings might represent numerous progressions: past to future, separate to unified, inner world to outer world, and so on.

The swirl design in Figure 7 (page 33) offers many creative opportunities. It has a fluidity that invites images of movement, play, and transition. It can be seen as four swirls, two ribbons crossing with a twist at the center, or three paisley drops flowing clockwise.

The mandala in Figure 8 (page 34) invites rich imagery that might suggest the cooperation and smooth functioning of separate elements. The mandala also implies a certain amount of stability within forms that are normally unstable. The use of color would help place the areas of primary interest and give the shape either great movement or great stillness.

BUILDING YOUR OWN MANDALA

Purchase a square piece of high-quality poster board or Masonite. Poster board is easier to use than Masonite, although it will not last as long. It can usually be found in the color you want and will not need painting.

If you use Masonite, paint the smooth side either black or white. Spray paint is fine as long as it goes on smoothly without any large drips. Artist's acrylic paints usually work best, although it is important to avoid excess drips or heavy brush strokes.

The next step is to create a materials box—a box big enough to hold both partners' choices of photos, cards, pieces of letters, images from magazines, and anything else that might be used in the mandala. Select these items from your personal vocabulary of symbolism. To some a cat represents power, to others it represents relaxation. Some see water as a symbol of the unconscious, while

FIGURE 1

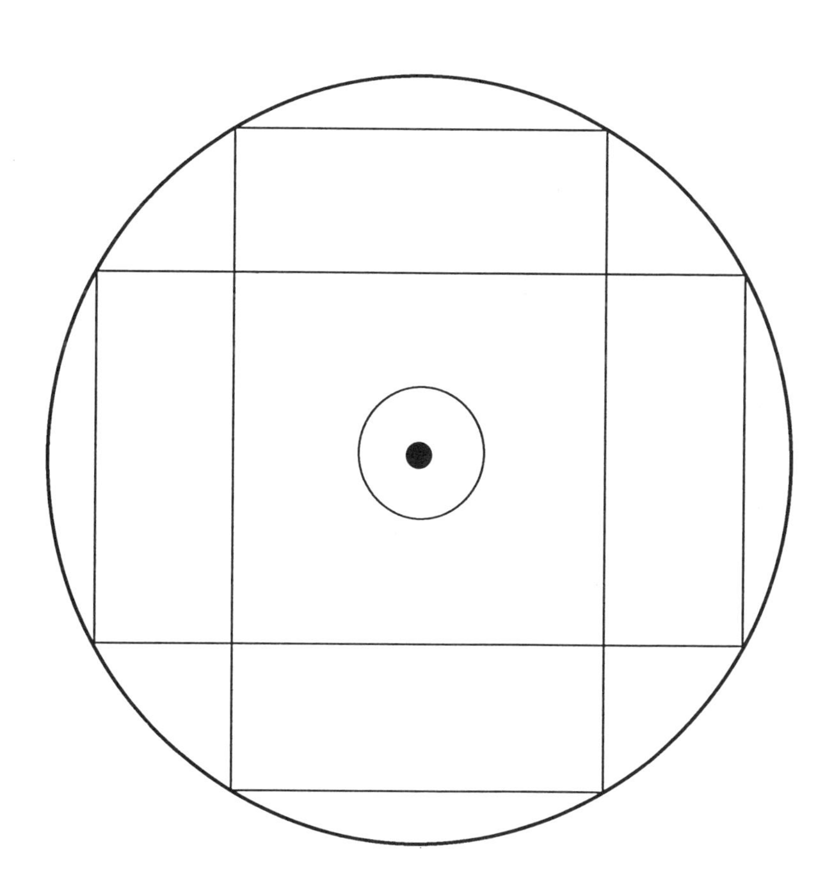

FIGURE 2

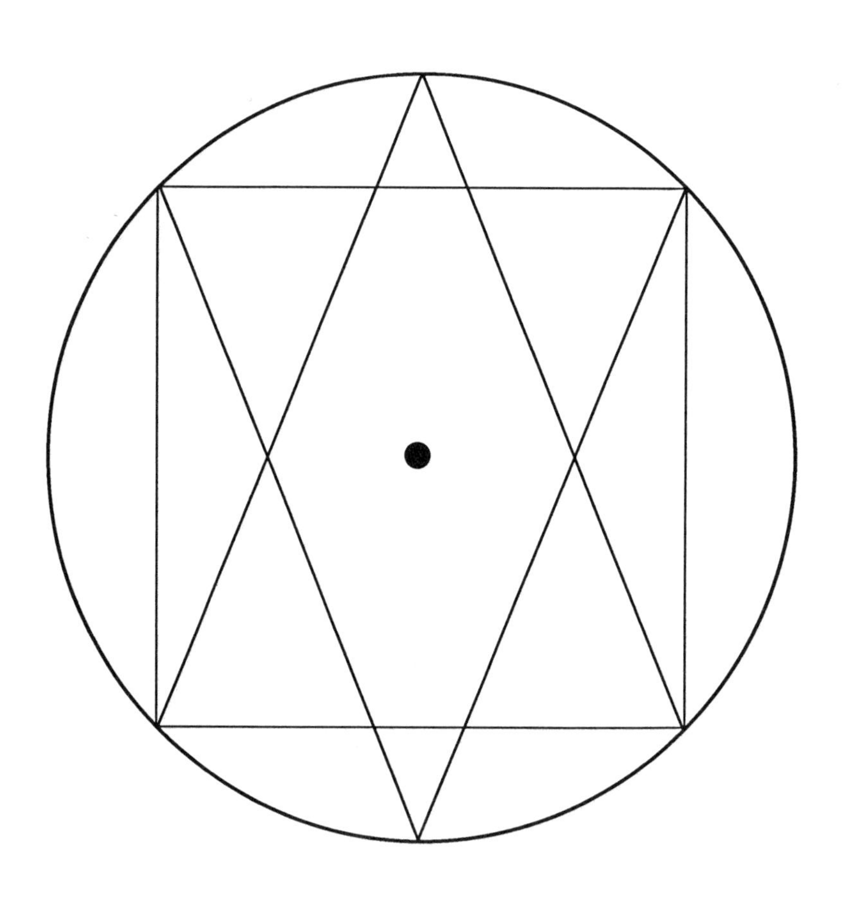

FIGURE 3

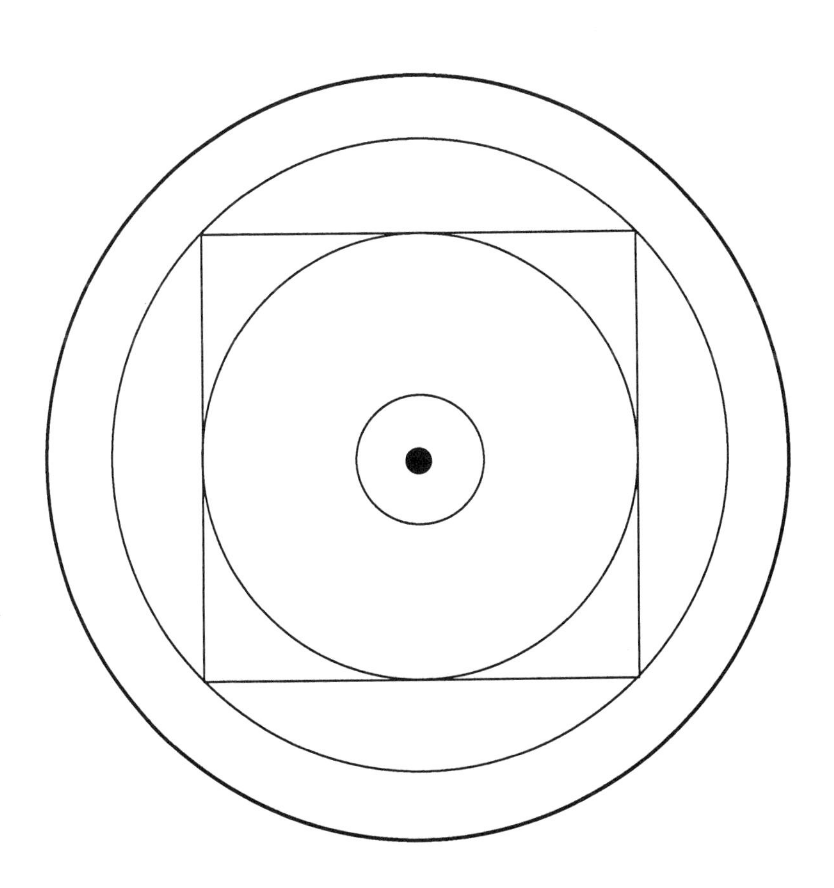

FIGURE 4

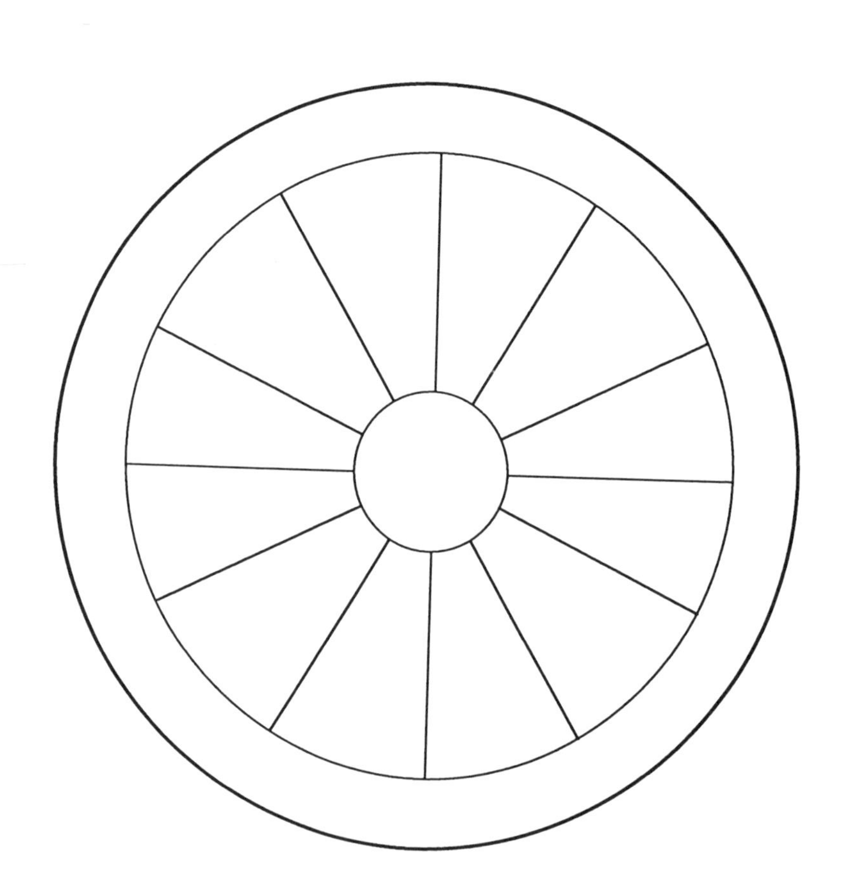

FIGURE 5

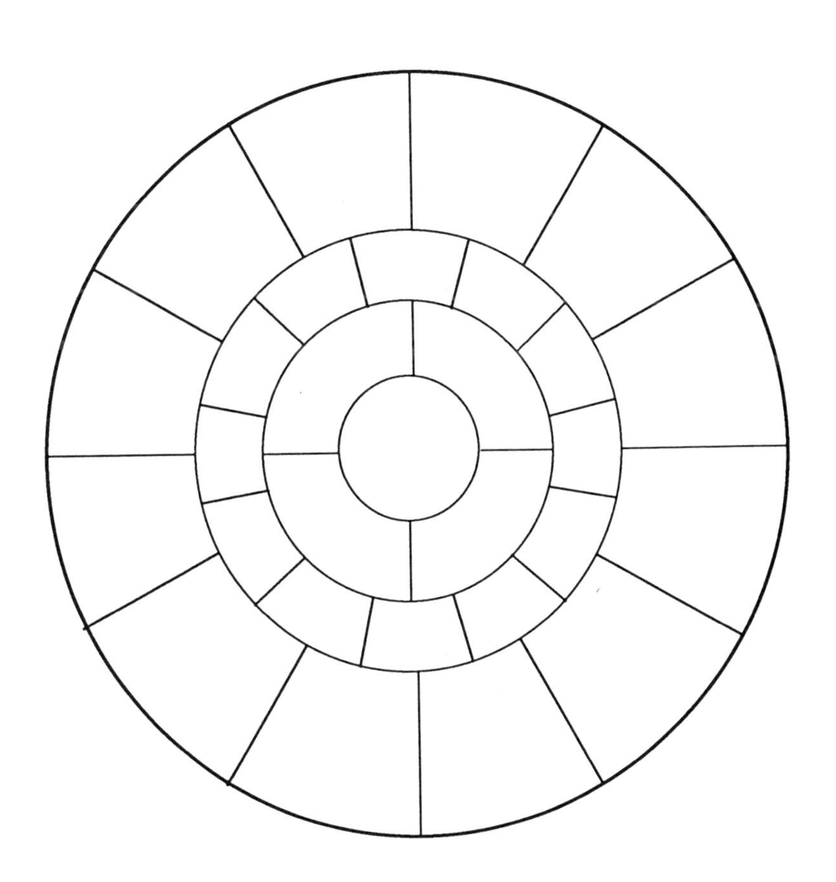

FIGURE 6

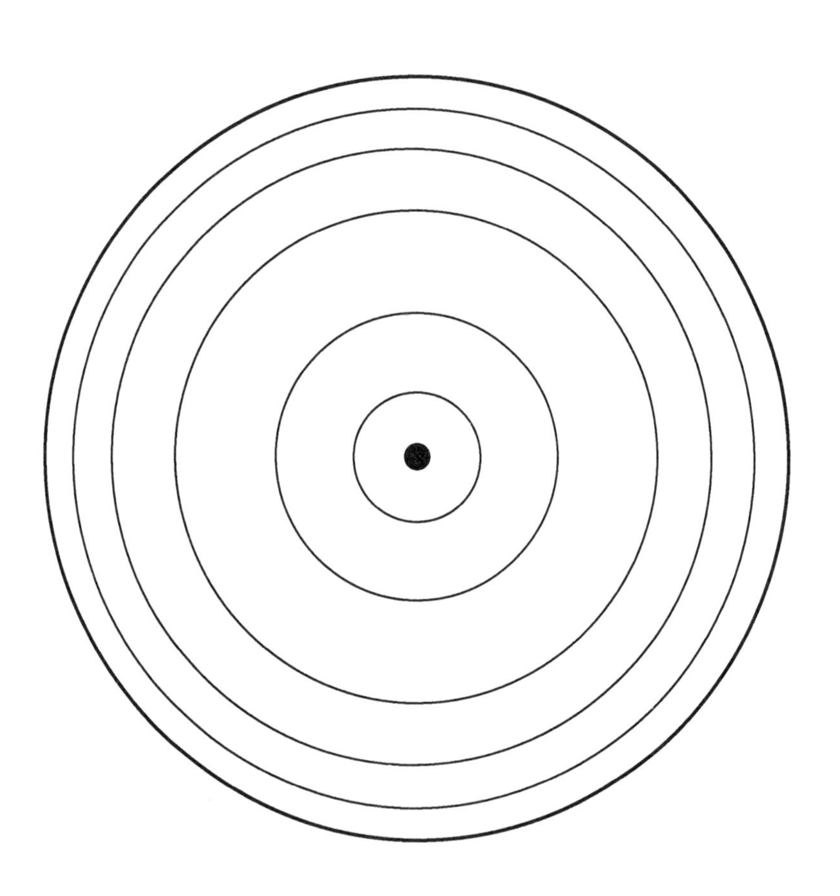

FIGURE 7

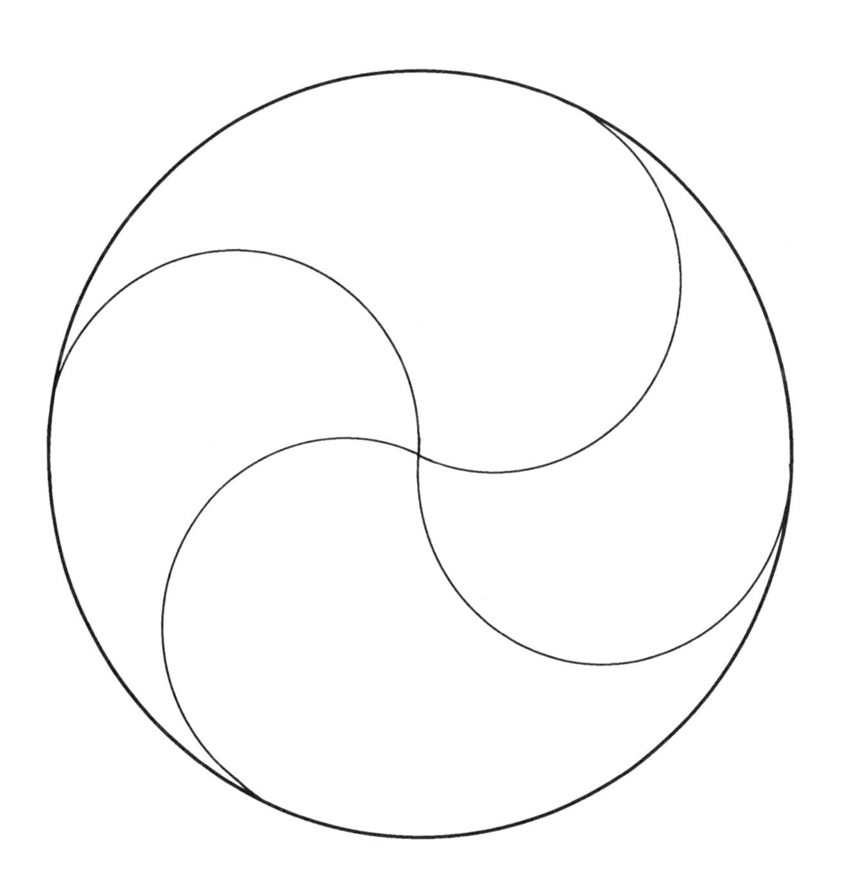

FIGURE 8

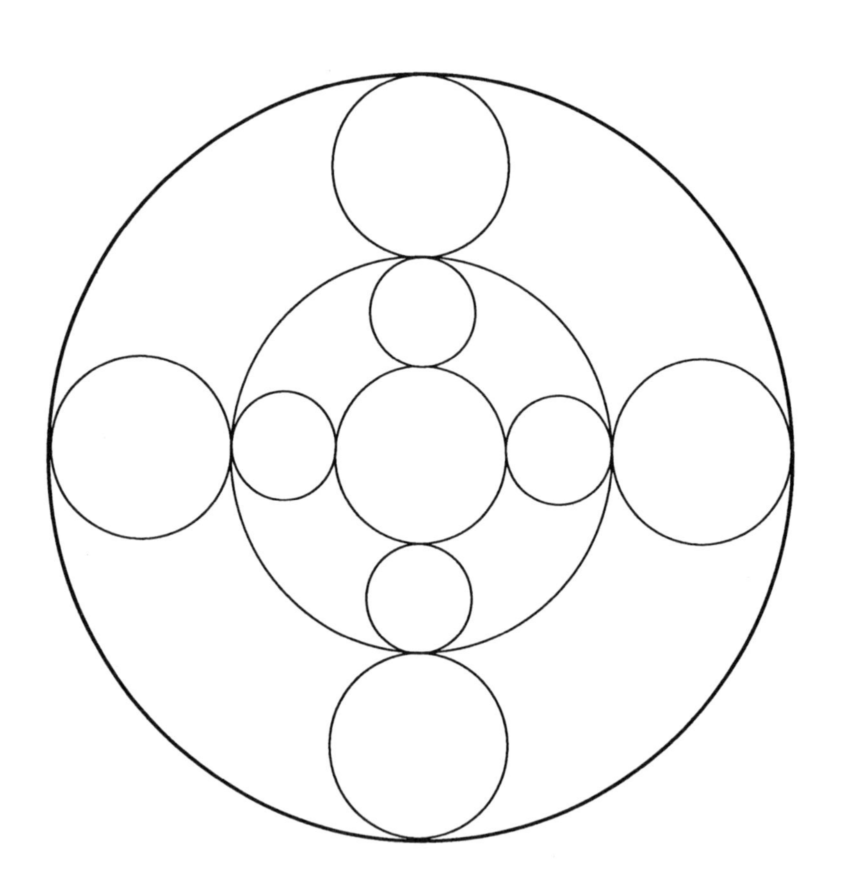

others see it as representing rebirth or one's sexual nature. The images one chooses need not fulfill any external expectations or traditional interpretations. If you sift through old photographs, for example, you will notice certain elements that appeal to you and seem to stir feelings related to conscious conception—feelings about family relationships, memories of childhood experiences, and so on. Gather any and all materials that seem even remotely pertinent. Too much material is better than too little.

You may find that certain images seem to consistently surface when thinking about particular aspects of the mandala. If this happens, you might want to go to the bookstore or the library to locate an artistic representation of the image, or try using your own art supplies to create a facsimile. Keep all of these images handy for inclusion into the design of the mandala.

There may be select words, phrases, or whole verses of poetry that come to mind when selecting items for your materials box. These verbal symbols can be included as they are or, if preferred, they can be translated into a visual representation.

While this box of goodies is taking shape (usually over the course of two or three days), begin to draw the mandala you have chosen onto your board. You must first decide on the scale of the mandala. If it is too small, it will limit your ability to express yourself. If it is too big, it will take too long to construct and will invite overstatement and repetition. A good basic size of 36 inches by 36 inches will usually result in a mandala that looks and functions quite well.

Assuming you have a workable square, measure the board to find the exact center and place a dot there to mark it. Next, take some measurements to determine the diameter of the circle. (You will probably want to leave a border of about two inches to allow for framing or matting.) Check all four sides of the board to make sure the edge of the circle is not favoring one side. Use a large compass, or whatever comparable device you care to invent, to help you draw the circumference of the circle. A push-pin with a string extended from it is a good tool, but make sure the string stays taut or the circle will appear wobbly. If you are drawing on black, use a white marker to create the lines. We suggest first drawing in pencil to rehearse and check your accuracy.

Once the circle is completed to your satisfaction, begin to draw the internal design of your chosen mandala. Be sure to check all measurements and keep all dividing lines straight. Because we are positively affected by symmetry and balance, the optic geometry of a mandala is as important as the content within.

Once the mandala has been outlined onto the board, both partners should sit in front of it and look at it in silence for a few minutes. If you have not done so already in the process of selecting a mandala shape, begin now to discuss what you envision in each subdivision of the mandala.

The Design

Using paints (again, acrylics seem to work best) and whatever items have been collected in the materials box, begin to collaborate on the design elements and the various emotional levels you wish to include in your mandala. This process can be quite fun. For partners who do not enjoy painting, gluing photos and magazine cutouts is an expressive alternative. The reverse is also true: If magazine cutouts seem too time consuming, you may want to try painting.

One section of the mandala might be designated to represent the love between the parents. This section might be painted in a color that both of you agree represents your love, or you may choose a color that combines your individual favorite colors or a color that reminds you of the day you fell in love, and so forth. Within this section you might place images of lovers depicted by famous painters, snippets of love letters, sections of photographs of the two of you, symbolic patterns representing your romantic love, a portion of a map depicting the site of your honeymoon, or any combination of words and images that best relate the humor, depth, complexity, and joy associated with your love.

Another section might deal exclusively with the concept of the ideal home. Here the images might be abstract representations of the warmth, harmony, and prosperity you want to achieve. The images might be represented by photographs of actual homes you admire or photos of past homes that evoke warm memories. The point is that, regardless of the section title or attribute, there are no limits to the representation of the ideas associated with it.

Work together in whatever fashion suits you. The main thing to remember is that you must honor the section boundaries and the center of the mandala. All else is open to your own artistic inspiration. Like all artistic endeavors, there will be some elements that are purely aesthetic, some that are purely meaningful, and many that are both. As long as both partners are pleased with the results, the balance of aesthetic versus meaningful imagery is immaterial.

Creativity is often enhanced by limitation. A fun game to play that works within this principle is to get an egg timer or some other reliable timekeeping device and sit opposite each other with your own collection of art supplies. Keep the mandala in the middle and set the timer for one minute. At the signal, begin to work on the section of the mandala immediately in front of you. At the end of one minute, each partner must stop instantly and move quickly to the next section. Start the timer and begin working again. Keep going in this way until you have completed two revolutions of the circle. You will be amazed at the results!

Another game, and one that is much less pressured, is to work individually within an artistic dialogue. One day only one partner works, keeping the results hidden until the next day when the other partner works. This process can produce some interesting and lovely results, especially if the partners view their individual work as a gift that will be awaiting the other the next day.

Just as valid, however, is the free-form method in which each partner works spontaneously at whatever pace feels right. A partner might contribute only one line, one tiny shape, or even nothing at all during the work session. The only guides at this point are sensitivity to the other's artistic needs and fidelity to the mandala.

The Finished Mandala

The mandala must be treated with special care at all times. Give it a place of honor to hang or rest while not in use. When in use, be sure to keep it clear of any food, dirt, or pets. By giving this kind of care and attention to the mandala, you acknowledge its significance and thereby add to its power.

The finished mandala is an aesthetic tool, a visual window through which your combined efforts are seen and actualized. The clarity and ultimate value of this window greatly depend on the degree of commitment and concentration of both partners.

The images you have included in the mandala work on your subconscious mind and interact with your deepest levels of thought. Your attention to the images gives them an added charge that can overpower negative thoughts and help maintain your focus on the conception process while dealing with daily events. The hopes, dreams, depictions of love, and elements of honesty that have gone into the mandala become imprinted in your visual memory and begin to expand outward into your actions in the everyday world.

It is important to allow the mandala enough flexibility to keep it viable. After the initial rendition is complete, it is appropriate to make occasional alterations, substitutions, or improvements later on. The mandala can and should be enhanced throughout pregnancy. New images may arise and demand to be included, more effective design elements may be found to replace less effective ones, and some details may turn out to be distracting or no longer applicable. Consider the mandala an ongoing process that only reaches its state of completion with the arrival of the baby.

MANDALA MEDITATIONS

The purpose of any meditation is entirely dependent upon the intent of the meditator. Some people are drawn to meditate by the promise of supernatural powers; some hope to alleviate stress and others hope to experience the mind in a state of complete stillness, free from the distractions of the world.

The following meditations promise no special effects, no instant cures, and no guarantees of escape from worldly distractions. Instead, they are presented as a means to fully integrate the many symbolic and nonsymbolic aspects of the mandala. The colors, symbols, words, and images within discrete sections of the mandala may be easily comprehended individually, but as a whole the mandala can be somewhat overwhelming. These mandala meditations allow the mind to accept, store, and fully integrate the many pieces into a coherent whole. They also offer the opportunity to focus the mind on the goal of a conscious conception by providing a situation in which the heart can fully resonate with the beauty of the entire process.

If time allows, both partners may want to experience the meditations together. Shared experiences like these are terrific bonding events and allow for discussion following the meditation. Meditating together, however, is not absolutely necessary. Individual meditation sessions can be just as satisfying. Regardless of the conditions of meditation, it is helpful to keep your individual notebooks nearby so that important impressions or insights resulting from the meditations can be recorded.

Meditation: Optical Focus

Place or hang the mandala so that it faces you at eye level as you sit in a simple meditation posture. (This posture could be as basic as sitting up in a chair to allow the spine to lengthen.) Next, focus your eyes on the center of the circle and hold your gaze steady as you breathe deeply. Detach yourself from the information stored in the mandala for the moment and simply observe the optical effects produced by the arrangement of shapes and colors. After a time, close your eyes and work to recreate the basic shape of the mandala on the inner screen of the imagination. Do this several times until you can hold the image steady in your mind for at least 10 full seconds. You will soon discover that you can maintain a steady image for longer and longer periods. Limit each meditation to 20 minutes at first to allow the mind to rest. Upon returning to normal consciousness, your breathing will stabilize, and you will most likely feel refreshed.

The optical focus exercise is a good beginning meditation because it acclimates the mind to the discipline of focus. It also challenges the mind to activate its powers of faithful reconstruction of observed reality. Because the meditation is free from emotional or intellectual discourse, it establishes a structural understanding of the mandala which may allow for some surprising insights.

Meditation: Image Cinema

Recreate the meditation environment as described in the optical focus meditation. Rather than limiting your gaze to perceive structural patterns, focus directly on the internal segments of the mandala, viewing them as doors to the imagination. Focus on one area and allow yourself to go deeply into it. Let your imagination experience that particular segment as if it were coming to life. Melt into it and explore it from all angles. Whatever images are stored in that section, allow them to affect you, to speak to you, to play out a film in your mind's eye, and to imprint a multitude of important data on your soul. Do this with as many segments as you wish.

This exercise often reveals a great deal of deeply humorous and sometimes deeply disturbing material. Regardless of the particular content and impact of the meditation, the selected areas of the mandala will now hold deeper significance for you. The insights gleaned from the experience can also enhance your appreciation for life's many facets and clarify personal desires related to any single facet. It is not uncommon to have insights that are as philosophically engaging as a personal definition of love and as practical as a detailed visualization of the ideal nursery design. These forays into selected areas are usually creative and always fun.

Meditation: Kinetic Mandala

The kinetic mandala meditation can be especially effective for those who enjoy movement. Place the mandala in a prominent position in the room and step back a few feet to allow for ample movement space. Let your breath be influenced by the variety of visual stimuli presented in the mandala. As you breathe with the mandala's visual rhythm, gradually incorporate movement of your arms, head, torso, pelvis, and legs. Explore movement possibilities with isolated parts of your body as suggested by the mandala, or use your entire form.

Your movements do not have to fulfill any preconceived notion of form; simply interpret visual information through your body. Words, sounds, or even songs are all acceptable additions to this meditation. Remember that stillness is an important part of movement. Give yourself the freedom to fully express your kinetic interpretation with the greatest range of movement you desire.

Movement patterns often emerge as a result of this kind of physical exploration. Refine these patterns until they become personalized movement hieroglyphs. These psychophysical symbols become endowed with the power to evoke profound emotional and mental connections to the mandala. When you have found a sequence of sound and movement that internally represents your mandala, you have completed a self-generated dance of love—a series of psychological gestures capable of transporting you to deeper states of creativity.

The purpose of the dance is up to you and your partner. The literal embodiment of the mandala is a worthy aim, as is using movement to imprint the data of the mandala onto your deepest self. Other equally valid aims must retain the force of your own invention. Remain true to your ultimate aim of inviting a being into your life.

3

PREPARING THE NEST

Humans, like all creatures on earth, have strong innate impulses that emerge once a child has been conceived. The woman usually responds to these impulses more readily and with more intensity than the man. She is guided by a series of complex biological changes within her body and by the expectations of her family and culture. These factors greatly magnify her nesting instinct.

For most women, pregnancy is an initiation into their natural wisdom. As they listen to their bodies, they experience an individual sense of maternal authority; they experience strong waves of expectation charged with powerful feelings; their lives become motivated by a deep sense of purpose.

Although imbued with the instinctual urge to protect and provide during these early stages of pregnancy, men tend to be somewhat disoriented by the process, reacting with uncharacteristic clumsiness in the face of nature's power. Nevertheless, a man is usually charmed by the changes in his partner's body and by the newly acquired radiance of her face.

Some unfortunate and ineffective behavioral tendencies have, over time, led to the procrustean cliché that says that women participate in the mystery of birth and men stand by awaiting the outcome. Luckily for both sexes, these rigid sociological boundaries are rapidly melting away, giving newer, more conscious tendencies a chance to thrive.

Men can now feel free to enact those nesting instincts not limited to protecting and providing. Women, too, are encouraged to follow their true nesting impulses, including the protecting and providing efforts previously claimed by men. One's own authority in these matters is rapidly becoming the most effective guide for women and men.

Naturally, the greatest degree of nesting occurs after conception is confirmed. There is a general gathering of resources and support for the big event. Nesting activities usually take the shape of buying a crib, preparing the infant's room, and getting showered with gifts useful for the care and comfort of the child.

There are some advantages to engaging in nesting rituals even before conception. Early nesting efforts differ somewhat from the more traditional preparations; they are practical and valuable yet they involve very little material accumulation.

PHYSICAL HEALTH

The first step in early nesting is the consideration of the physical health of both partners. Improvements in health aid fertility and help the couple endure the early months of child care. If either partner regularly indulges in alcohol, the period prior to conception is a sensible time to eliminate it, at least for the duration of the conception and gestation periods. This is particularly important for women because alcohol can be detrimental to the developing fetus. Both partners are advised to stop smoking, as tobacco impedes the growth of the baby. In fact, all unnecessary stimulants or drugs should be eliminated during this time. Reduction of sugar and caffeine as well as saturated fats is suggested. Consider this to be the ideal opportunity for a physical cleanse. You want the blood and organs to be free from toxins, and you want to be in top shape.

If you have access to a good nutritional consultant, physician, or holistic practitioner who can prepare a thorough food allergy analysis, it is well worth the investment, especially for a mother whose milk might reflect those allergic traits: While the mother may not suspect a food allergy, experiencing only a mild reaction after eating a certain food, the nursing baby often inherits the same allergy. When the refined particles of that food are ingested through the mother's milk, the baby may experience strong discomfort.

Physical conditioning is an important early nesting consideration as well. Vibrant physical health translates into enthusiasm for life and for the creation of a new life. The commitment to health is a commitment to life, to having the energy and love necessary to go the full journey of raising children. Invest the time and energy into a good cardiovascular and muscle-toning program. The benefits can be wonderful.

PSYCHOLOGICAL HEALTH

The next step in early nesting efforts is to build a healthy psychological foundation for conception. Take a thorough inventory of your current behavioral foundation and, if it is strong, build onto it. People who believe they have strong behavioral foundations received good parenting values from their parents, from parental figures, or from their own resources. A strong behavioral foundation implies that both partners feel good about becoming Mom and Dad, and they feel ready to adopt their own parenting model. (One method for conducting a thorough overview of your behavioral foundation is to work through the questions provided in the personal inventory worksheet later in this chapter.)

A strong foundation not only relies on time-tested family traditions but also has built-in flexibility that makes one capable of adapting to the traditions of the partner's family. Realistically, however, psychological foundations of this ideal strength are few and far between.

Most couples today begin with a desire to redefine their models of parenting. If both partners work outside the home, for example, they may desire creative ways to smoothly integrate the new family dynamic into their lives. If their opinions differ about raising children or about religion, finances, politics, domestic duties, responsibility and freedom, and so forth, they may assume that all differences will be resolved by their enduring love. Unfortunately, the divorce rate speaks for itself. The alarming number of divorced families serves as a warning about building futures on unstable ground.

What then can become the foundation for a new humanity—a humanity where children emerge whole, focused, clear-eyed, and prepared for their own journeys into the adventure of parenting? The answer lies in one word: honesty. The strength to admit fear, to recognize personal shortcomings, and to acknowledge destructive patterns is one part of this honesty. It is equally challenging to have the strength to admit happiness, to recognize personal talents, and to acknowledge the resourceful and creative patterns that already exist in each of us. This kind of honesty is the deepest form of love. The heart soars in this atmosphere of clear, unromanticized reality.

Strengthening Your Psychological Foundation

A personal inventory is the first step toward achieving the honesty called for in this conscious conception work. Unadorned views of one's self provide rare and refreshing data necessary for the creation of a solid psychological foundation. When this step is completed, it becomes easier to achieve the next step: an honest look at the world around you.

Scrubbing away the blurry belief systems and notions perpetuated by family and social conditioning can be a formidable task. Some people invest in years of therapy to arrive at this state of clarity and personal authority. By investing the time and effort during the crucial period of preconception nesting, you might save yourself future counseling.

Using your individual notebook, answer the questions in Figure 9. State your honest reactions and feelings, not the reactions you habitually use or think you should say. Be positive, but do not be afraid of negatives—they are the grist, the fuel, and the material to be transformed. Allow this to be an intimate exercise of total honesty.

Upon completion of the worksheet, review your answers and write a three- or four-paragraph self-description; that is, describe yourself to yourself in simple, honest terms. Then carefully review your answers and your self-description. Check to see if you have a penchant for either exaggeration or understatement, pessimism or optimism, avoidance or attack, or any other habitual thinking pro-

FIGURE 9: ***Personal Inventory Worksheet***

1. What are my earliest memories?
2. What are the elements from each memory that make me feel good, safe, or happy?
3. What aspects of parenting did my parents do well (warmth, education, humor, etc.)?
4. What aspects of my parents' style of parenting would I change or improve upon?
5. What kind of parent do I want to be? (Be specific. Include descriptions of exact scenes or exact words.)
6. What skills do I now have that will help me become this parent?
7. Who are the others in my life who make up a support system on which I can rely in times of need?
8. What do I now do that sustains my self-confidence, my self-reliance, and the creative control of my life?
9. What additional skills do I need to acquire?
10. What does the word *home* mean to me?
11. What things about myself do I like?
12. What things about myself do I wish to improve?

cess that may impede a simple, objective view of yourself.

Recognizing your personal self-image bias can go a long way toward allowing you to change if change is desired. More important, the act of clarifying to the basic ground of honesty is in itself a valuable step toward effective parenting.

While there are plenty of resources to consult concerning the larger subject of parenting, our intention here is simply to help you arrive at a state of fearlessness and clear vision about your wish to bring a child into the world. Keep in mind that nobody is perfect. The personal inventory worksheet is not designed to be a self-flogging tool—it need not be moribund and gloomy. Rather, the process is meant to clear away any outstanding self-delusions and bring you to a deeper, more mature level of responsibility regarding conception and parenthood.

It might be helpful to consider that, at its most essential level, parenting is the process of guiding a child by means of example and unconditional love so that he or she is ready to begin the life adventure. As simple as that may sound, however, it is actually a very difficult and complex proposition requiring enormous resources of patience, understanding, and team effort by both partners.

Once the individual perspectives begin to focus, it is time to consider the combined tasks at hand and ahead. The next step in this direction is to go beyond personal issues to marital ones.

Fully discuss with your partner the issues presented in Figure 10. Take them one at a time and exercise total honesty without fear of judgment. Allow ample time for each issue, and when conflicts arise, write down the nature of the conflict on a separate sheet of paper and go on. Do not dwell on the points of conflict at this time.

FIGURE 10: ***Issues for Discussion***

1. How many children do we want?
2. Do we want a hospital or home birth? Midwife, doctor, or both?
3. What environment do we want for the baby's birth?
4. Will father attend the birth?
5. Will we have natural childbirth?
6. Will mother work during pregnancy? After birth?
7. Will we have sex during pregnancy? Up until what stage?
8. Are we aware of and prepared for the changes in our sexual lives during pregnancy and following the birth of the child?
9. Will our child breastfeed? For how long?
10. Will we use cloth diapers or disposable diapers?
11. What are some career changes or adaptations we may want to consider for ourselves?
12. Ideas for keeping the romance alive?
13. What is our parenting style (control versus free-form)?
14. How will child-care duties be shared?
15. What is the religious framework for our family?
16. Should we have a will drawn up?
17. Do we start a trust fund or savings account for our child?
18. Are we interested in public schools? Private schools? Home schooling?
19. Do we want a traditional or alternative medical approach?
20. Do we want a pediatrician or a family physician?
21. What other private issues need attention?

Later, after all the issues have been discussed and a few days have passed, address the areas of conflict. It is important that each partner respects the ideas and concerns of the other. If a subject seems emotionally loaded, you can diffuse the emotional charge by refocusing on the goal. Keep things in perspective, and remember that a difference in opinion is not an issue of right or wrong—it is a matter of style. Work to find compromises that result in a win/win situation for both partners.

Keep a record of your individual feelings, reactions, and choices regarding each issue. After arriving at compromises and agreements, record them in your personal notebook. This gives you easy access for future reference when related conflicts arise or when values change.

Consider again the mutual affirmations of love and partnership. Recall the vows of marriage in whatever form they were expressed. Refresh each other's memories about the sparkling moments of love that still live within your hearts. Keep the flame of romance alive by creating surprising situations that will deepen your love. Accept that you both will age, change, and go through many transformations together. Distill to the essence the love you have for each other and reaffirm in writing or in person your commitment to that love.

Sweeping clean the inner terrain will help prepare the outer. As always, humor keeps things in perspective. There is no need to have any fear—most parents will tell you that the rewards far outweigh the pains of parenting.

PREPARING THE STATEMENT OF INTENT

The exercises in this chapter have laid the foundation for you to formulate your statement of intent. You now have ample data to write your individual statements and to create a combined statement.

Set aside an evening to present some or all of your writings to each other. Include your statements of intent as part of the presentation, which can be as simple as reading aloud from key passages, sharing photocopies of select pages, or exchanging notebooks. Afterward, work together to merge your two statements into a single, coherent statement that represents the essential aspects of each. Write the combined statement into the master notebook.

INNER VISION: FOCUSING

As a final touch to this work of preparing the nest, find a comfortable spot to sit, close your eyes, and review the work on self-image. See yourself as a parent completing some of the tasks outlined in the personal inventory worksheet. Endow your image with strength, warmth, and love and then see yourself holding your child in a sweet, gentle embrace. Take a deep breath and as you exhale, sigh into the scene you have created. Bask a moment in the glow of the scene and then release the image and open your eyes.

4

THE INVITATION

Few couples actually take the time to invite an unborn child into their homes. Particularly in today's world, people are so busy with their pursuits that they overlook this aspect of the process of conception. The invitation is, in fact, the most important step, because it is during this time that a whirl of mysterious forces begins to shift and arrange itself in response to the combined inner states of each partner. The field of potential energy begins to respond to you like a plant tilting toward the sun.

There are many systems of thought that attempt to demonstrate this notion. Some rely heavily on religious symbolism while others attempt to explain it scientifically.

Regardless of the point of view, it seems clear that commitment to a single idea or state of being has enormous power. It transforms the cognitive imperative of individuals and at times appears to interface with the laws of physics.

The making of a mandala, as described in Chapter 2, is a good representation of how the combined impulses of two people can come to a fixed center. The mandala serves as a reminder that by integrating your inner sensations and desires around a conscious intent, the myriad complexities of the world begin to align and respond to your actions.

Up to this point, the conscious conception work has prepared the nest in many material and nonmaterial ways, gathering data and delving into personal imagery. As partners you have developed a deeper bond and a sense of purpose by working through the process. Now, with heartfelt focus on the invitation, you are metaphorically drawing the circle of the mandala. The power of this act creates a vortex of energy and an unforced vacuum that invites by its very nature.

WRITING THE INVITATION

Think of your invitation as a homing beacon for your potential child. To activate the beacon, each partner must write a formal invitation in your individual notebooks.

Using your own tone and wording, be sure to thoroughly consider the following points:

1. State your reasons for deciding to invite this child. This could be as simple as "It was the time," "It felt right," "We knew we had a lot to offer this child," "We felt ready to be parents," "We wanted to make a contribution to the world," "We want to build a family," and so forth.
2. Express the love and care you already sense for this being.
3. Describe dreams or images that have surfaced (include both past associations and recent ones).
4. List what you hope to learn by being a parent. Some men hope to learn to be communicative fathers. Others wish to experience the joy of childhood again. Some women long for the strength of motherhood, others for the chance to learn how to nurture. There are many possibilities.

This part of the invitation is designed to remind the parents that you too are sharing in a learning event and that, although your role as parents will certainly include teaching the child, it will also include the child teaching you.

Share nothing of your statement with your partner. At this stage privacy is important. These topics are subjective and may take a good deal of inner searching; therefore, each partner requires the freedom to search without fear of judgment or expectation.

Allow at least three days to complete your individual invitations. Keep in mind that these invitations, and indeed all of this work, should neither be rushed nor allowed to slowly drag on. Find a workable time frame, but regardless of the amount of time you have allowed, live the moments fully. Concentrate completely. You know you are working at the right level of focus when time becomes elastic.

Once the individual invitations have been created, meet at a specific time and share your writings with each other. We suggest reading aloud to create the ideal opportunity for both partners to reveal the deep feelings and warmth they feel for their combined futures. If you choose to read the invitations aloud, make sure to write legibly or type the invitation so your partner does not have to stop and ask for translations.

Your invitation is a pronouncement of love for life, learning, and the adventure of parenting. Ultimately, it is an affirmation of a very special commitment to the long-term caretaking of a beloved new being.

As a result of its emotional nature, tears of joy, swells of love, and waves of trepidation may accompany this exchange. Be careful not to become too self-indulgent, but feel free to give full rein to these emotions. Their expression develops an honesty that invariably becomes material for more effective communication.

Unexpected elements of humor may also surface. Savor these, as they are an essential part of your natures as well as a healthy way to deal with tensions and fears.

After the individual invitations are shared, write a third invitation that combines the two. This newly created invitation should express the couple's shared vision yet remain true to the essentials of the individual invitations.

It is sometimes necessary during this part of the process to discuss areas of apparent conflict. Most conflicts can easily be resolved through careful listening; that is, each partner should listen to the other's invitation as if it were his or her own. Remain open for compromise. As conflicts get resolved, incorporate their resolution into your combined invitation.

Place the combined invitation within the master notebook, which may also hold the writings of each partner that support the invitation theme. These entries might include dream images, poetry, drawings, quotations, or anything else that expresses the heartfelt desire to invite this child into your home. Create a closing statement that sums up, perhaps in metaphorical terms, the essence of your combined commitment, your abiding love, and the joy you feel as you anticipate the arrival of your child.

PRESENTING YOUR INVITATION

At a special ceremony of your own design (preferably late in the evening before going to bed), hold hands and read aloud the new, fully integrated invitation. The ceremony could be as simple as sitting in silence for a few moments before the reading, or it could be as elaborate as arranging background music, candles, or loving movements to accompany the event. Keep distractions to a minimum.

This session is a device to gather the focus and blend the intentions of both partners into a single, unified intent. The combined invitation is like a marriage of thoughts and feelings. It is the contract of love that endows the marriage with a new strength of purpose. Speaking the words aloud is important, because it aligns thoughts with breath and feelings, planting the invitation in the body as well as the mind. Voicing the words of the invitation can be a powerful experience when you do so with the sensation that you are actually speaking to your potential child.

DIRECTING YOUR THOUGHTS

Begin to incorporate positive thoughts about the child into your daily lives. Take a few minutes of daily meditation to reflect upon the kind of being you hope to attract. Be sure to record all significant thoughts and dreams in your individual notebooks. Your days will soon become highlighted with the glow of your loving invitation.

The incorporation of positive thoughts into your daily activities may produce a number of changes almost immediately. For example, many mundane tasks may begin to seem brighter, clearer, and somewhat sweet. The invited child may appear in the dreams of either one or both parents, an especially propitious indication that the invitation is being received on a deeper level.

It is also likely that your expanded awareness will result in a noticeable reflection of your interests. You may begin to see a lot of babies whereas you used to see very few. People may relate their baby stories to you, and the books you read, the music you listen to, the television you watch—virtually every aspect of your life—will begin to participate in this new adventure.

As the signs of contact with your invited child become more numerous, you may begin to feel an array of new sensations ranging from uneasiness (as though someone were watching your every move) to a feeling of intense happiness (as if you were supported by the whole universe). These and all other related sensations are natural and should be accepted as part of the adventure.

WELCOMING THE CHILD

When it becomes clear that conception has indeed occurred, feel free to celebrate, congratulate, and give thanks. These moments may well be uncalculated, bursting forth from the natural flow of thoughts and emotions. Allow the spontaneous joy to play out completely—dance, laugh, cry, write love notes, paint pictures—do something with all that energy. People close to you will most likely be swept into your enthusiasm as well.

Some people have their reasons for relishing the news

in private, opting to inform friends and family after several months. This is perfectly valid and has its advantages. For example, a couple may wish to continue their nesting preparations without being interrupted by excited friends and family.

Regardless of your approach, immediately begin to relate to the new being that has begun its journey into biological life. The invitation was accepted, and the guest will soon arrive—now make him or her feel welcome.

Be forewarned: The realization that conception has occurred sometimes produces unexpected moments of depression. Powerful childhood memories may surface and trigger the release of repressed emotions. Allow these moments their time, but avoid indulging in them. Instead, refer often to the mandala you and your partner have constructed. Release what needs to be released, but keep your eyes on the aim at hand and on the love you have for this child you have chosen to invite.

INNER VISION: THE MEETING

Choose a position you can comfortably sit in for a while, and close your eyes. View the backs of your eyelids, and watch the play of light and shadow. Gently shift from this screen to your inner screen where you can use your mind's eye to perceive a swirling globe of light.

Hold this ball of light in your mind's eye for a while, then gradually allow the light to form into the image of a baby. Do not try to force the vision in any particular direction; let the scene, any scene, unfold. At some point, let the baby look directly at you. This can be a good opportunity to reinforce your invitation to let this being know it is welcome and to invite it into your life with all of your heart.

This is also a good opportunity to listen. Let the baby speak to you through words, gestures, thoughts, or any other mode of communication. Try not to edit or obstruct any impressions during these exchanges.

Finally, let the form of the baby return to a swirl of energy. Let the swirl dance in your vision for a few moments and then gently bring your attention back to your eyelids. Slowly open your eyes, and record the contents and impressions of the visualization in your notebook.

5

SEX AS ART

When human endeavors reach a refined level, we call it craft. When craft reaches a level of uniquely expressive refinement and is endowed with great purpose, we call it art. Sex as art is an intimate communion between partners that blends a wide variety of impulses into a single act of loving communication. To fully experience the beauty of conception, one must approach sex as an art form. The mandala, the nesting preparations, and the invitation are all part of this process of expression and refinement.

Before sex became the complex marketing, legal, and medical issue it is today, it was seen as a symbolic act of cosmic union. The energy of sex was considered to be sanctified as the blissful vibrations of the unity of opposites. This is true in the Hindu, Tibetan, Taoist, and Hebraic traditions, to mention a few.

Sex is predominantly viewed by Western society today as a mechanical biological act, an advertising tool, a source of domestic intrigue, or a medical risk. The romance and beauty of sex, particularly as it relates to procreation, is almost entirely ignored.

Too often sex is used by the media in an exploitive and sensational manner to achieve effects that translate into profits. The constant barrage of today's portrayals of sex tends to distance sexuality from true intimacy and move it toward fashion and consumerism. Attempts to rectify this imbalance usually take the form of repression (blaming sex itself) and result in moves to institute neo-Victorian standards of behavior. Ironically, modern efforts to reclaim intimacy would be more effective if they were to borrow from the wisdom of most ancient traditions.

The act of sex is obviously the means by which organic conception is achieved. From another perspective, sex is a highly charged electromagnetic event that quickens the vibrational force of the body and dramatically shifts the physical energy field. It is an event not unlike that which occurs during other peak experiences, such as artistic inspiration or religious epiphany.

This highly charged vibrational event could be metaphorically described in sound: It is the haunting cry of the Hebrew shofar, the joyful ring of a church bell, the pulsing ring of the Tibetan singing bowl; it is the great song of creation resonating and calling forth. Perhaps sex is indeed a kind of signal, an electromagnetic event, similar to the release of sound waves, that creates a vibrational ripple on the subatomic level and contacts another vibrational field—one destined to become a human being, a being that was inexorably attracted by the vibrational tone, so to speak, of the call.

Clearly, there is no scientific proof to verify or deny this concept. Instead, science has managed to give us a detailed outline of the exact biological events that occur in the conception process. The details, although useful in terms of dispelling superstitions, are little more than a description of the mechanics of the process. At this level, it seems clear that the cherished pleasure of sex could be reduced to a means of ensuring the continued survival of the species.

Although scientists are finding locations of coded information on the DNA, they have no idea how the information is constructed in the first place or from where it originates. The plain fact is that we do not understand the forces that create the egg and prepare it for fertilization or that drive the sperm to fertilize the egg.

Sometimes if we divide things into their components, the elusive obvious reveals itself. Let's try it: The egg and the sperm are cellular constructions. Cells are clusters of molecules, and the molecules are clusters of atoms that are themselves made up of immeasurably small electromagnetic wave particles. Each component has its instructions to build and maintain the next component.

By the time we reach back to the components of waveform particles, we are out of the world of standard physics and fully into quantum physics where the laws of order are quirky and unpredictable. At this level, space and time become tricky and the previously ordered, hierarchical components no longer fit into modular constructs. It is vibrational wonderland.

Consider what we know about vibrations affecting other vibrations: When middle C is struck on a piano, for example, all the C strings move in sympathetic vibration. Now consider that the electromagnetic activity of the brain communicates constantly with the cells of the body, maintaining life functions, healing wounds, and relaying states of fear or security.

With that in mind, could we imagine that the enhanced vibrational frequencies attained during sex affect other frequencies within and even beyond the confines of the body? We do, in fact, give off continuous brain waves and other oscillating frequencies just by being alive. Is it conceivable that a chord of energy achieved through the thoughts, feelings, and sexual expressions of a couple could awaken a sympathetic chord somewhere in that quantum wonderland? Could this vibration affect the formulation of the atoms which form the molecules which form the cells which form the zygote which grows to become a fetus and later a child?

Based on the available data, this idea is at least a remote possibility. Therefore it follows that the work of conscious conception, including the sexual act, has the potential to formulate coherency within the vibrational field.

How do we enhance the sexual ritual for maximum coherency? How is it possible to filter out the pornographic, abusive, and commercial aspects of sexual energy and maintain the positive, blissful vibrations that transform sex into a loving, conscious communion?

One possible solution, and one that has been used by numerous ancient religions, is to experience sex as a form of meditation. There are many styles of meditation familiar to most people: chanting, dancing, prostrations, sitting in silence, reading from holy scriptures, prayer, and so on. Any one of these forms could obviously be enacted in nonmeditative ways. What, then, makes it a meditation? The answer, quite simply, is the activation of sincere inner focus.

This inner focus is an essential technique behind the Tantric practices of Oriental cultures, where primal energy is gathered during sex, generating great resources of vibration which are then used to raise the individual to higher states of perception, such as deep compassion, visionary insight, and love. These states are made possible by directing the organism to refocus the energy resonated during sex.

Through purity of heart, the meditation ritual of sexual union between two partners who are prepared to accept a child into their lives can reach rarely experienced, exalted energy states. The intensity of their union, sparked by specific intentions to invite a being into this dimension, transforms sex into a conscious act, a work of art.

PREPARING THE EXTERNAL

To begin this beautiful process, it is important that each of you honor your individual needs as well as the needs of your partner. The following procedures are not set in stone. Adjust them to match your honest, innermost needs.

Both partners begin by participating in a ritual cleansing of the bedchamber. There are practical concerns in this cleaning ritual, of course, but the greatest value comes from the bond established through the shared work that honors the bedchamber. Make the bed with fresh linens, dust, remove clutter, and decorate—all delightful tasks when performed with a sense of purpose. Be careful, though: Overdramatizing this ritual can distract from your true aim. Keep it simple.

Next, begin to create mood factors within the chamber. These can take the form of incense, candles, music, essential oils, or anything else that you and your partner find pleasurable and appropriate.

Do only what is essential to alter the ambience of the room from the familiar to one with a heightened atmosphere, one of intentional beauty. Draped fabrics, paintings, and special lighting are effective. If music is used, the selections should be mutually agreed upon and arranged so they do not need constant attention. Use candles of good quality, new enough to have an even burn, and place them on a safe, protected surface. Maintain sincerity with these mood factors, but avoid becoming sanctimonious.

PREPARING THE INTERNAL

Once the external factors are established, consider the internal mood, a highly personal and very important aspect of the entire creative act. Emotional moods are mercurial and fleeting; they are too complex for conscious control. Think of mood, therefore, as a mental state, a relaxed sense of communion and fun.

A ritual bath is a good place to begin working on the internal mood. Bathing each other by candlelight can be a wonderful experience. Use scented bath oil and plenty of warm water; then apply after-bath lotion to each other while still in the bath chamber.

Other rituals to enhance inner mood might include massage, singing, or even something as simple as snuggling together. Some couples need time to just gaze into each other's eyes. Some want to dance together; some want to talk over a cup of tea. Each couple is unique, and the chemistry of their love is unique. You and your partner must decide together the kind of inner ambience you hope to achieve. We encourage you to use meditation, dance, prayer, readings from inspirational books, or anything else of your own invention that could help make the internal transition to the appropriate mood.

What is the appropriate mood? Again, this is highly personal. It may be helpful to think of it in musical terms: You are creating a purifying series of notes that have the potential to create sympathetic vibrations with the exact corresponding notes in the invisible realm. These melodies are all songs of love, of course, and by first tuning the internal mood to a particular music, the external elements of the actual intercourse will provide a form of amplification for this inner music.

The amplified music of this event, combined with the other elements of preparation, may establish a frequency that can attract a particular soul. Relax and trust that the clear and open surrender to the loving resonance of your shared erotic love can orchestrate a veritable symphony. You will both become composer, player, and listener, inviting a new being to enter the music and renew the themes of human life.

INNER ALIGNMENT AND LOVEMAKING

It is possible for both partners to consciously align themselves with their higher purpose during the act of lovemaking, providing helpful guidance for a being's transition from the infinite to the finite dimension. As previously suggested, an appropriate mood should be established and shared by both partners. Staying well within this mood, couples are invited to participate in one or more of the following exercises.

Focus 1: Attunement

This attunement exercise suggests ways to attune to each other moments before the actual act of coition.

In a bedchamber, preferably at night and using only candles to illuminate the space, sit close together, comfortably facing each another on pillows or chairs. Each partner should be nude or seminude. In silence, begin to scan your partner's body with your full attention. Concentrate on the details and generate a sense of love and respect for each part of this organic form. Allow moments of arousal to occur. If you are stimulated by seeing a particular part of the body, take that sensation and imagine you are painting your partner's entire body with that feeling, using areas of visual stimulation as a palette of energy that you may dip into and spread across the entire form. When you have completed this exercise, bring your attention to your partner's eyes.

Now touch hands. Let the hands begin to dance, to explore, to express erotic tenderness. They can clasp, stroke, tickle, glide, rest, wiggle—using all manner of movement in heavy or light modes, on and on in an unending interplay of sensation and communication.

Keeping the hands connected, link your energies across the space, synchronizing your breathing rhythms. Once this has been accomplished, keep the eyes engaged and begin to sense filaments of light extending from your body and hooking up with filaments from your partner's body. Make sure the forehead, neck, chest, stomach, pubis, and feet all have strong, stable links.

At this point the two of you have created the basis for profound coherency of feeling and attention. Maintain your intensity of attention and allow it to sharpen even more. Within given moments you may feel a new level of energy between you. While maintaining your eye contact and other visceral links, allow for the possibility of moving together into a variety of postures. Resist the temptation to lead each other; instead, breathe together and allow the kinetic link to lead both of you into a variety of sensations and postures.

There are no correct or ideal postures to seek. Your purpose is to maintain linkage and allow for the postures to emerge naturally from your combined energies. Some postures will be mirror images of each other, some will be distinctly different. Some will remain near the floor while others may ascend to a stand. Let this slow dance of inner alignment continue until you both, quite naturally, stop and resonate in one singular posture.

Then, when it feels right, move together to the bed. Once there, and maintaining full attention, let the flow of energy lead you quite naturally and even playfully into the first gentle exchange of kisses and strokes.

Focus 2: The Flow of Light

The Male Partner.

Visualize a channel of light pouring into your heart while you are engaged in intercourse with your partner. Let it spread to coat your entire body. Next, visualize the light as collecting in the testicles and charging the sperm with consciousness. As the energy builds to a climax, visualize the light as concentrating in the penis and finally shooting out in golden bursts.

The Female Partner.

Visualize yourself as the "source of life" while you are engaged in intercourse with your partner. See your womb as the wellspring of the future. Visualize a channel of light that pours into your heart; let it spread to coat your entire body. Next, let the light collect in each ovary and extend down the tubes to meet the cervix. As the energy builds to a climax, visualize golden light pouring into your deepest self. Stay attentive to any particular colors that may flash into your mind or any particular fragrances you may suddenly smell—signals that conception may have taken place.

Focus 3: The Song of the Breath

While engaged in intercourse, allow your breath to arrive at a synchronous rhythm. Both partners may inhale and exhale together or alternate the breath—one inhales as the other exhales. The point is to fulfill the breaths in long, slow, simultaneous strokes.

Let the entire experience of lovemaking harmonize with the rhythm of your breathing, providing a sensation of being rhythmically "locked in." As the natural rhythm of the experience ebbs and flows, allow your breath to follow suit, maintaining a simple pattern.

This synchrony has the effect of lifting and stabilizing the current between the partners, creating a state of blissful union. Maintain eye contact or bring your foreheads together as the energy flows through the entire system, further linking the two lovers and making it easier to stay in harmony.

You may experience fleeting visions of texture, light, color, or design while doing this exercise. Sometimes the room, your partner, or both take on a luminescent quality. Although these visual effects are certainly pleasant, do not be overly distracted by them. Instead, maintain a pure connection to the breath and the flow of energy.

Next, begin to sense the breath as sound. It does not have to be limited to the sound you can produce yourself, although that is certainly an appropriate match in this circumstance. Let the inner ear unhinge itself from its rational moorings for a moment, and allow it to participate in the breath, receiving sounds on a deeper level as well.

Each person may experience a different kind of music during this stage. Some people might not experience music at all, at least not in the conventional sense. Others might hear an entire symphony, a wondrous song, or a series of simple, blended sounds. Whatever the experience, avoid judgment and interference by the controlling mind; instead, plunge into the energized sea of sound, guided by the breath.

As the rhythm of lovemaking intensifies, it is not unusual for the couple to experience the same inner song. It is also not unusual to participate vocally to some degree. At the moment when the rhythm of synchronous breathing becomes unmanageable, allow the breath its full freedom, listening all the while to the unfolding inner music.

AFTERWORD

At the very least, the exercises in this book can stimulate couples to clearly articulate their wishes to themselves and to each other—a significant step toward growth as individuals and as partners. At the most, these exercises can begin to upgrade the manner in which human beings are brought to this plane of existence.

Day-to-day involvement with this work will help to integrate it into the fabric of your day-to-day reality. In this way, you may experience life with morc depth and come to a renewed appreciation and respect for the simple gifts we often take for granted. As the wise ones say, however, be careful not to mistake the finger for the moon. In other words, avoid thinking that these exercises are any more magical than your own sense of innate wisdom.

We urge you to continue working with the notebooks and the mandala and to use the positive visualizations during, and even following, the pregnancy. During pregnancy it is useful to relate to the developing fetus as a conscious being, expressing love and respect for your child's journey in its liquid dimension. Sing songs, read poetry aloud, caress the womb/belly, and take time to listen to the presence of this emerging intelligence.

Partners can participate in a considerable amount of prenatal playing with their baby: Tap out rhythms, provide gentle massage, swim, place the mother's enlarged belly against the father's belly and then listen together to the movements of the fetus, and laugh—laugh a lot.

Mothers will naturally have a strong connection with the child and may at times need to enter moments of deep, silent communion. On the other hand, the father may need to adopt a caring, supportive role and connect through overt means. Talk to the baby, listen to the womb, and make things for the infant-to-be. The father-to-be should also take extra care to appreciate the beauty of the maternal belly. The mother may need reassurance that her bountiful size is also beautiful and desirable. Invest in at least one maternity outfit that has some style. (Bonus points go to the mate who either buys such an outfit or goes with his partner to pick it out.) Above all, this is not a time for the man to be selfish. Instead, he should seize the opportunity to demonstrate his support, love, and domestic competence—or at least a grand sense of humor and spirited sportsmanship.

The female system is busy nurturing the offspring. One normal by-product of this magnificent endeavor is a tipsy hormonal balance. As a result, emotions tend to flash and flow for unusual reasons and cravings come and go. In fact, the entire spectrum of behavior suddenly becomes available to the woman during this time. It can be exciting, hilarious, and, of course, frustrating.

As the moment of birth nears, both partners need to reassert their love for each other and for the adventure upon which they have embarked. Something as simple as a foot massage can do wonders for both partners. Reading through the master notebook is also helpful.

Certain sacrifices will inevitably accompany parenthood, and it is a good idea for both partners to be clear about their capacities to sacrifice. It is important to know not only what you are willing to sacrifice but also what you are not willing to sacrifice.

The sacrifice of energy is one universal and inevitable sacrifice of parenthood. It takes enormous amounts of energy to be a parent because, quite simply, parenting is a lot of work. If both partners recognize, however, that they can draw vast resources of energy from their shared love and from the presence of their child, the energy will flow more easily.

The partners must also recognize that their dynamic as

a couple will soon become the dynamic of a family, where roles change, bodies change, priorities change, and the entire marriage relationship changes. Throughout these shifts, it is important for the couple to maintain a healthy vision of their child, their relationship, their home, and the birth itself. Transition on any level requires conscious adjustment. You may take courage in knowing that working toward a conscious conception can go a long way toward providing a bond strong enough to withstand the winds of change.

We recognize that in today's world there is a growing number of alternatives to the traditional family. There are single-parent families, extended families, adoptive families, and gay- and lesbian-parent families. This work does not exclude these nontraditional families—the principles presented here apply regardless of the family conditions. It is important for those who wish to invite a child into their lives to do so consciously, to become effective and caring parents, and to create healthy, safe, and loving homes.

Keep in mind that conscious participation in conception is not an attempt to forcefully engineer the birth of a child. Instead, it is a conscious relationship with natural law. The power of this relationship must be handled with the utmost care. While we may benefit from an interface with the laws of creation, we must always remain respectful of the greater, more powerful workings of nature.

We wish you much love and prosperity in the years ahead.

INDEX